The Phosphorous Grove

Aflame with Love Upon the Witch's Tree

by

Christopher Penczak

COPPER
CAULDRON
PUBLISHING

Credits

Words & Art: Christopher Penczak
Layout & Publishing: Steve Kenson

For more information visit:
www.christopherpenczak.com
www.templeofwitchcraft.org
www.coppercauldronpublishing.com

ISBN 978-1-940755-09-0

Second Edition, Printed in the U.S.A.

AZOTHTOZA

To Rosaria,
May you find your way to the grove
and burn with love eternal.

Contents

Introduction

The Phosphorous Grove is my most unusual work to-date, harkening back to my days of lyrics and song writing, rather than metaphysical texts. In those days, I felt overwhelmed by the spirit of the song, the idea would have me on fire, and I would furiously write in a little notebook and record bits of pieces of melody on a small hand held tape recorder meant to record office memos. They would come in the dead of night, in the car, in class and in all manner of inconvenient times. When my life as a musician, or at least as an active song writer in a band was over, a different inspiration flowed. I learned to channel some of those impulses into the art of ritual and extend the flow of creativity into books.

It took a time of immense emotion and turbulence to bring this flow of poetry back to me. From when my mother was on her deathbed due to complications from a long dance with cancer and the various treatments meant to help, and for the few months after she passed, I was strangely on fire with an inspiration. In the hospital, in the middle of the night, in the car, I was on fire. These little short mystical verses came out. I had to get three or four of them on paper until I realized they were somewhat Qabalistically based, using a more Witchy version of the Sephiroth and Paths connecting them.

These poems flowed up the Tree of Life, and were infused with the images of Witchcraft, Alchemy and Hermetic Qabalah. I soon arranged them in order, and began reciting them prior to meditations. They provided a powerful focus and the images came to life. I shared them on social media, and felt that the response by those who "got it" was strong. I shared them in my fourth degree Witchcraft class, focused on climbing the Tree of Life, and while only a few used them meditatively, those who did blossomed. So I am sharing them here and now, in a very special limited edition book of poetry and art.

I offer this work to both my Mother, and to the spirits of the Temple of Witchcraft in the form of this fundraising hard cover edition, to help us ground our dream of a Temple in the physical reality. She encouraged my musical and magickal bouts of inspiration with unending support, and has been a metaphorical mother for many of us association with the Temple teachings and traditions over the years.

In the end, I realize that the poetry itself paints a picture of the eternal sabbat of the Mighty Dead, the phosphorous grove where we are all aflame with love, will, and wisdom. May it be a humble roadmap to get you just a little closer to the Timeless Tradition.

Blessings,

Christopher Penczak

Full Moon, November 2013

Malkuth

KINGDOM & GARDEN

TERRA

EARTH - AIR - FIRE - WATER

KNOWLEDGE AND CONVERSATION
OF YOUR WATCHER

The Kingdom of the Garden is where
the Queen rules supreme
As the throne of Understanding made manifest.

Only through courting her four daughters
does the Knight-King fulfill his Sacred Trust
And resolve the Mystery of The Sphinx,
Turning the harvest wheels.

Camelot rises from the ten stones
and descends again under the waves.

Path 32

to Yesod

TRUMP XXI

THE UNIVERSE

SATURN

TAU

CROSS

Living only in the Pentagon Room of the Senses,
Learn to open and close all five doors
And rise through the All Mater.
Taught that No Gods Exist, in both senses,
We still seek the Pater beyond all existence
And in our seekings find the sixth secret door
And She of the Three Ways.

Path 31

to Shod

TRUMP XX

THE AEON

PLUTO

SHIN

TOOTH

The sky is not falling but the heavens
open their vaulted gates.
Time marches forward and cannot be stopped.
The unreal becomes real
and we rise beyond our limitations,
Tried by fire and smoke.
We enter the wizard's tower
and must now pay coin for the knowledge therein.

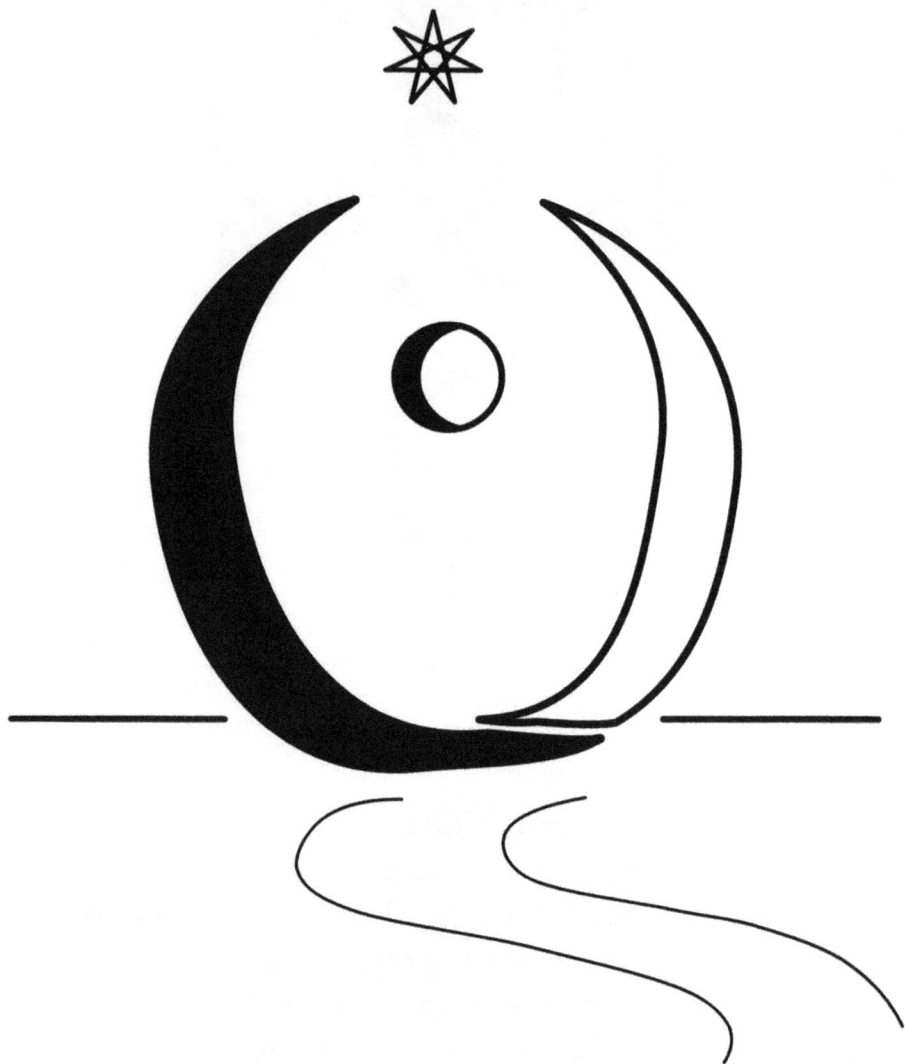

Path 29

to Netzach

TRUMP XVIII

THE MOON

PISCES

QOPH

DOOR OF DREAM

The Gate of Horn and Ivory
looms large before the heart.
Curved tusks, black and white towers,
form the Vesica Piscis.
Through this Yoni Eye of God
Leads the umbilical cord or hangman's noose.
Guarded and guided by the lupines
in the garden of the Moon.
We move past the illusions
To find the light of the Victorious Courts of She.

IX
Yesod

FOUNDATION

MOON

WATER

VISION OF THE MACHINERY OF THE UNIVERSE

Witch Moon. Moon Gate. Gateway. Way of the Night.
Open the way into the Mysteries.
Open the way to astral sight.

Trees both dark and light, severe and merciful
are alchemically transformed into the Witch's Willful
and Wise Heart to hold the door.

Do you hold the key within your soul even as She
waxes and wanes?

Rise up unto She who is the mirrored light of fate
and the nierika of the Anima Mundi.

Take your place among the stars.

Path 25

to Tiphereth

TRUMP IV

ART

SAGITTARIUS

SAMEKH

PROP

Cauldron. Forge. Fire burn. Water cool.
Magick rise unto me and remake me anew.
Temper the metals within me with your hammer.
Hone my edge.
Stir the waters within me with your apple wand.
Brew the philosopher's elixir of gold
plucked from Hesperides at the bottom of the sea.
Grow the seeds of wisdom
with your water that burns and your fire that flows.
Ishi Baha!

Path 28

to Netzach

TRUMP XVII

THE STAR

AQUARIUS

TZADDI

FISH HOOK

Stargazer.
Star Goddess.
Stars within the Heart of the Earth
reflected in the Vault of Heaven.
Pour out your cosmic nectar so I may rise up with hope.
Pour out your bright waters so I may open
the Witch's Heart of Love and Desire
Pour out the currents of the Aeonic flow
So I can fulfill True Will in all things near and far.
And be one with the Queen
of the Earth and Starry Heavens.

Path 30

to Shod

TRUMP XIX

THE SUN

SUN

RESH

FACE

Child of Light
be hidden no longer.
Sing. Dance. Play.
For the child of light show us the true way.
Connecting darkness to light and heaven to earth
Riding the chariot, the ark,
the steed of joy and mirth.

VIII

Shod

𝔐

SPLENDOR

MERCURY

AIR

VISION OF SPLENDOR

Splendid infinity in a grain of sand
that becomes the center still point
Within the lemniscate of every Temple Magister
turned Magus.

Weaving wonders, weaving words,
weaving webs within webs.

Taught by spider poets living in quicksilver strands
woven on the game board of life.

Each piece plays its part perfectly
until the game begins anew.

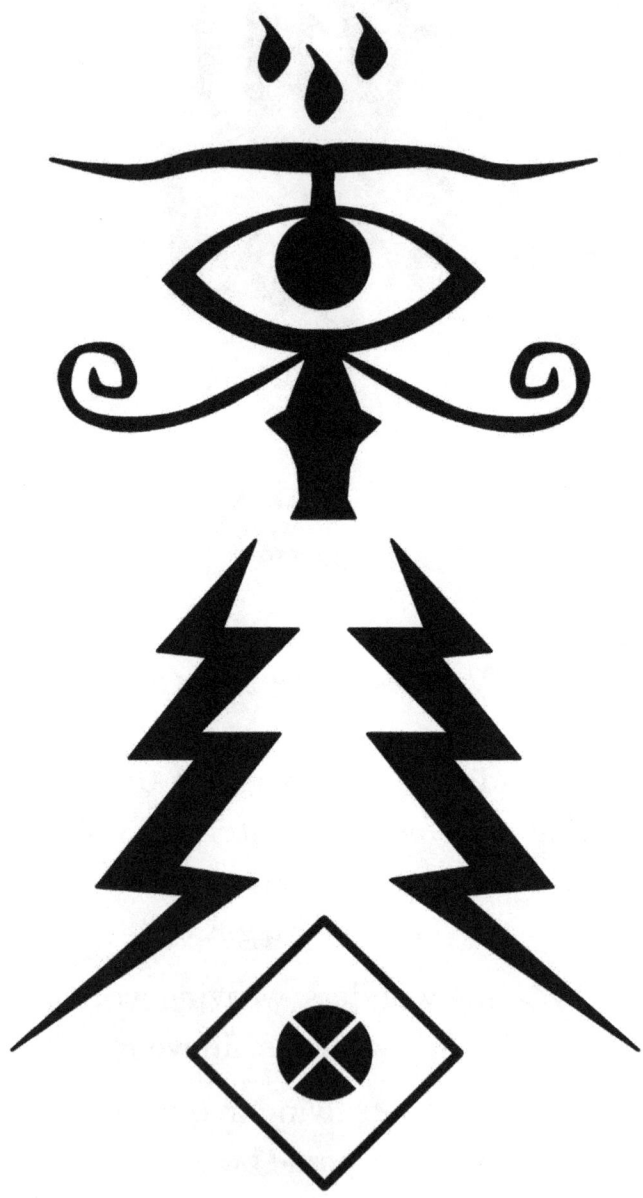

Path 27

to Netzach

TRUMP XVI

THE TOWER

MARS

PEH

MOUTH

Open the Eye that sees all that was, is and shall be.
Open the heart to change.
Open the mouth and ear to truth.
Experience the lightning strike
of Witchfire and Wisdom.
And come tumbling towards your foundation stone.
Begin again aflame with love.

Path 26

to Ciphereth

TRUMP XV

THE DEVIL

CAPRICORN

AYIN

EYE

Only those with the eyes to see and the ears to hear truly
Can perceive the Devil
Only those who notice the details of Baphomet can be
admitted into the Fields of Paradise.
Rather than run screaming blind to the horror,
Dissolve and coagulate your fears.
Cast off you leaden chains and follow the light.

Path 23

to Geburah

TRUMP XII

THE HANGED MAN

MEM

WATER

Hanging upside down. Hanging inside out.
Blood and psyche strewn across the fields
for all to see, yet none do.
Invisible. Immaterial. Insubstantial.
Drowning in our own sea of dreams.
See truly the Path of Unmaking.
Wake up and rise forth as a Gallows God.

VII
Netzach

♍

VICTORY

VENUS

FIRE

VISION OF BEAUTY TRIUMPHANT

Enter the Garden of the Gods and be as you ever are
in the Zep Tepi eternal.

Embrace the briar hedge of five fold balms and banes.

They will open their mysteries to you.

Seek the Verdant Queen below who ushers forth
emerald waves of life and love as her children.

It is here where we first find the bloom of the red rose
triumphant and know true beauty.

Path 24
to Tiphereth

TRUMP XIII

DEATH

SCORPIO

NUN

FISH

In order to truly live, you must die.
Seek death and be reborn under the grim rose banner.
Welcome death's touch upon your shoulder, ever advising.
Let these echoes of self rot away and fertilize the garden.
Become what you already are.

Path 21

to Chesed

TRUMP X

FORTUNE

JUPITER

KAPH

GRASPING HAND

The Namer walks the Rim of the Loom
The Watcher sits in the center.
The Shaper walks the strands like a spider.
Up. Down. And up again.
Turned by an open hand or a clenched fist.
It matters not.
Spin the Wheel from the center of the Web of Fate.
And become like the Weaver.

VI

Tiphereth

✕

HARMONY

SUN

AKASHA

VISION OF HARMONY & SACRIFICE

You are the Child of Light within
the heart of the Cosmos.

Hope and Harmony radiate from you into the darkness.

Do not forget the Child when you wear the golden
crown, for the Child and Sovereign are one and the same.

The sacrifice on the altar of the Watcher is of ego,
not innocence, and with sacrifice it is thus transformed
to copper-gold.

Path 22

to Geburah

TRUMP IX

ADJUSTMENT

LIBRA

LAMED

OX-GOAD

All are eternally lured by the call of equilibrium,
like the horse led to water, yet few drink.
Fill our cup with the waters of life
and seek True Will in all you do.
Rise up and though every shifting balance,
become one with true power.

Path 20

to Chesed

TRUMP IX

THE HERMIT

VIRGO

YOD

CLOSED HAND

Offer not pity to those upon the path.
Ultimately it is the poison of the clenched fist.
Only hold tightly to the Lamp of Illumination
that guides us onward.
Offer the open hand of compassion,
or the cords of mercy to lift up.
Do not fall back into the pit
and become trapped again.

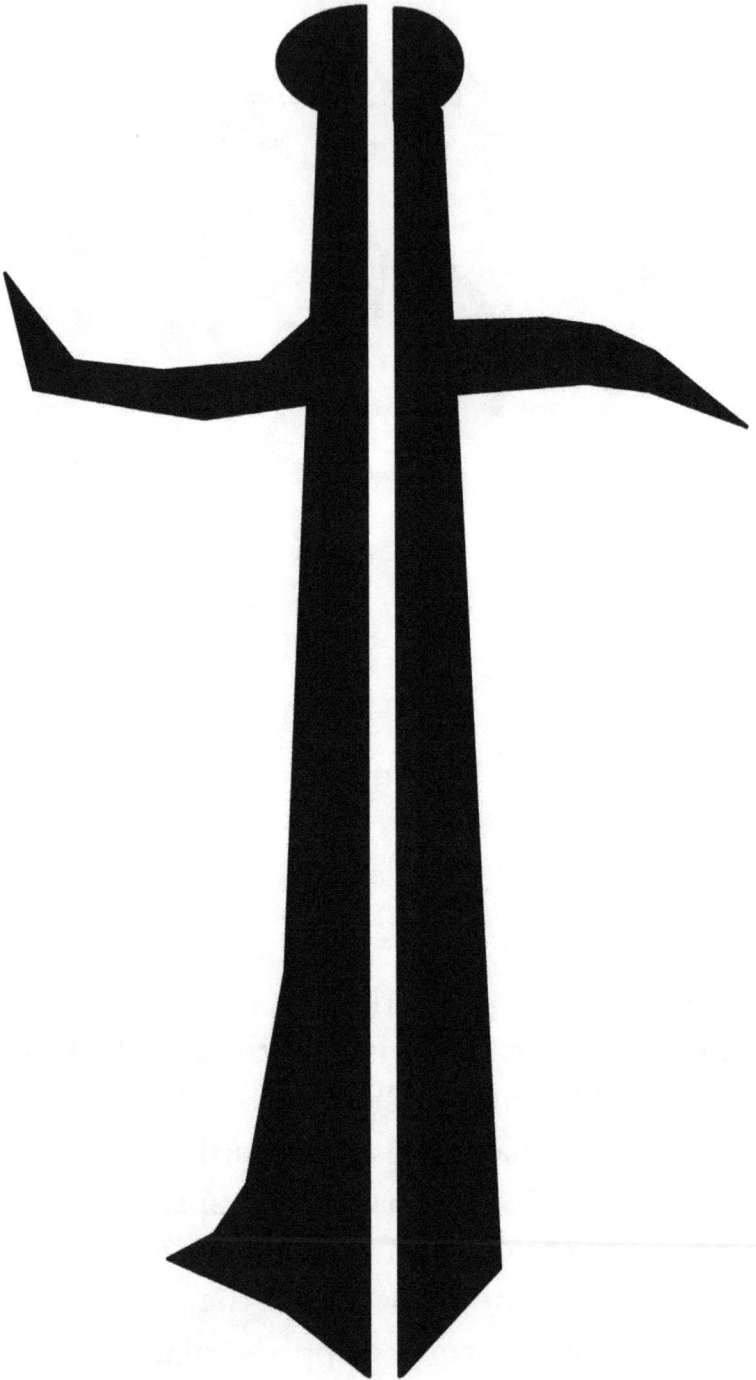

Path 17
to Binah

><

TRUMP VI

THE LOVERS

GEMINI

ZAYIN

THE SWORD

Across the razor's edge you will find
your lover in the mirror darkly.
Reflected in the curve of the universe
comes your double, your twin shadow.
Through the alchemy of the lion and the crow,
The Watcher puts forth the drawbridge knife
across the Abyss.
Will you walk it, and find love eternal?

Path 15
to Chokmah

>≈≈≈<

TRUMP IV

THE EMPEROR

ARIES

HEH

WINDOW

With the Witch's Eye gaze through
the Red Star of Might to the Father.
Gaze across the darkness to starry road.
Be mighty like dragons.
Be mighty like bears.
Be mighty like swans.
Be mighty and charge forward
toward the light of loving wisdom.

Path 13
to Kether

TRUMP II

THE PRIESTESS

MOON

GIMEL

CAMEL

The Chariot of the Goddess,
The crescent boat pulled by dragons, wolves, and silver stags,
Shall guide you across the Abyss of Eternal Night.
Wheels within Wheels of the Earth, Moon, Sun and Stars she spins.
Wheels within Wheels of the Belly, Head and Heart she spins.
All that you need to cross is now within your vessel of light.
Properly prepared you are.
She opens the veils to reveal the Paradise of the Garden beyond.
There you shall find the Land of Apples and Pomegranates,
burning with light.
There you shall dwell in the Zep Tepi,
the time beyond time, the space beyond space.
There you shall find the Phosphorous Groves
And that which dwells beyond the light.

Geburah

POWER & MIGHT
MARS
VISION OF HARMONY & SACRIFICE

Only through the ordeal are we properly prepared.

Are you prepared to suffer in order to learn?

Then all of nature and super-nature
shall rise up to test you.

Purified by She Who Strikes
in her fires of red, blue and gold,
all that no longer serves your spirit is burned away.

Stripped of almost everything,
burning with the flames of immortality,
you shall receive the five-fold world.

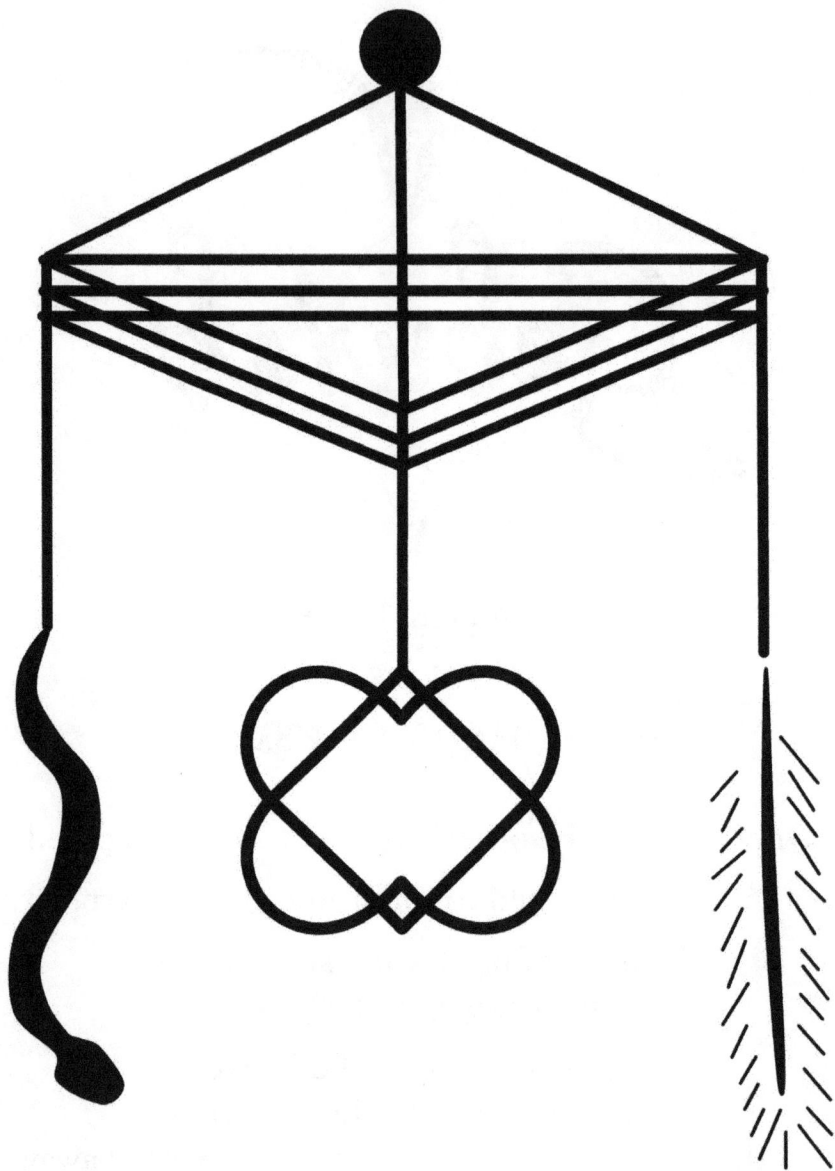

Path 19
to Chesed

TRUMP VIII

STRENGTH/LUST

LEO

TETH

SERPENT

Balanced by the Serpent Scale
Balanced by the Feather
Balanced by the Heart of a Master
One finds the still point where the impossible is possible
By staring into the possibility of danger
Yet possessing the strength and desire
to go forward regardless.

Path 18
to Binah

❦

TRUMP VII

THE CHARIOT

CANCER

CHETH

FENCE

Prepare the Vessel.
Prepare the Broom.
Prepare the Cauldron Chariot.
To enter the throne chamber of the Witch Queen.
Dissolve and Coagulate
By the virtues of the Lion, Bull, Dragon and Phoenix
within your shell.
Vessels within Vessels upon the Mountain.
Jump the Hedge of Unknowing and
pass the Veil of Concealing.
Ride the Waves of Creation.
In Preparation to Cross the Abyss.
Zazas, Zazas, Nasatanada Zazas

IV
Chesed

⊼

MERCY

JUPITER

VISION OF LOVE

Be crowned and conquering with the four pointed,
twelve starred crown of humility and pride.

Take residence in the four squared castle of the winds,
blowing from the dread Lords of Outer Spaces.

Reside beneath and between the jeweled web
of the Lady Weaver, reverberating with the
cosmic laughter of the Lord.

Path 16
to Chokmah

TRUMP V

THE HIEROPHANT

TAURUS

VAV

NAIL

Horned Priest of the Mysteries,
Give me benediction.
Yoke me to the stars and beyond.
Devil Priest of my Fathers,
Teach me rebellion.
Show me how to break the bonds of illusion.
So I may rise up to the Starry Heavens
While my feet are rooted in the Mother
of the Four Squared Castle.

π

Da'ath

❧

KNOWLEDGE
URANUS
VISION OF KNOWLEDGE ACROSS THE ABYSS

The beggar washes himself in the fountain
in the court of the infinite tower first
and is covered with dirt and grime.

Upon his return he washes again and is purified.

He is restored.

Every time we too reach upward to be clean and
drink true, we do not restore the apple to the branch,
but grow our own tree to new heights.

Together they stand until time and tide take us both
back through knowledge to the Source.

III
Binah

⚓

UNDERSTANDING
SATURN
VISION OF SORROW & JOY
MASTER OF THE TEMPLE

Burn with the black flames of the Goddess Saturnine.

The Mighty Dead wept tears of blood
into her cauldron cup so that we can wear
the dark feathered cloak of truth.

Now we fly through the Abyss
to weep the holy tears ourselves and burn.

Blessed be and be blessed in return.

Path 14

to Chokmah

TRUMP III

THE EMPRESS

VENUS

DALETH

DOOR

Mother Nature lifts her skirt and
opens her doors to let life in.
Mother Nature bares her breast and
opens her doors to feed her children.
Mother Nature holds out her arms and
opens her doors for us to return.
There is no end.
Life feeds life,
From the Beginning to the End.

Path 12
to Kether

TRUMP I

THE MAGUS

MERCURY

BETH

HOUSE

Through the Dread Door I have come
Through the gateway of the Mysteries I have come
Above and Below and Between, to return home.
Oaths taken. Gardens tended.
Measures taken and Weeds pulled.
In the holiest of holies,
In the circle between the worlds,
In the eye of the storm of souls
I make my dwelling always and forevermore.
By Light, Life, Love and Law I craft this house
And by Liberty I leave it.

11

Chokmah

✣

WISDOM

NEPTUNE

VISION OF SOURCE

MAGUS

Stars upon stars upon stars.

Gushing forth white upon black, forever un-gray,
swimming towards the heart womb of the Mother.

A King with no need for a crown but carrying
the Wand of Creation wisely, while
singing the Oran Mor, the Great Song.

By seed and flower comes the fruition
of the universe known and unknown.

Awen.

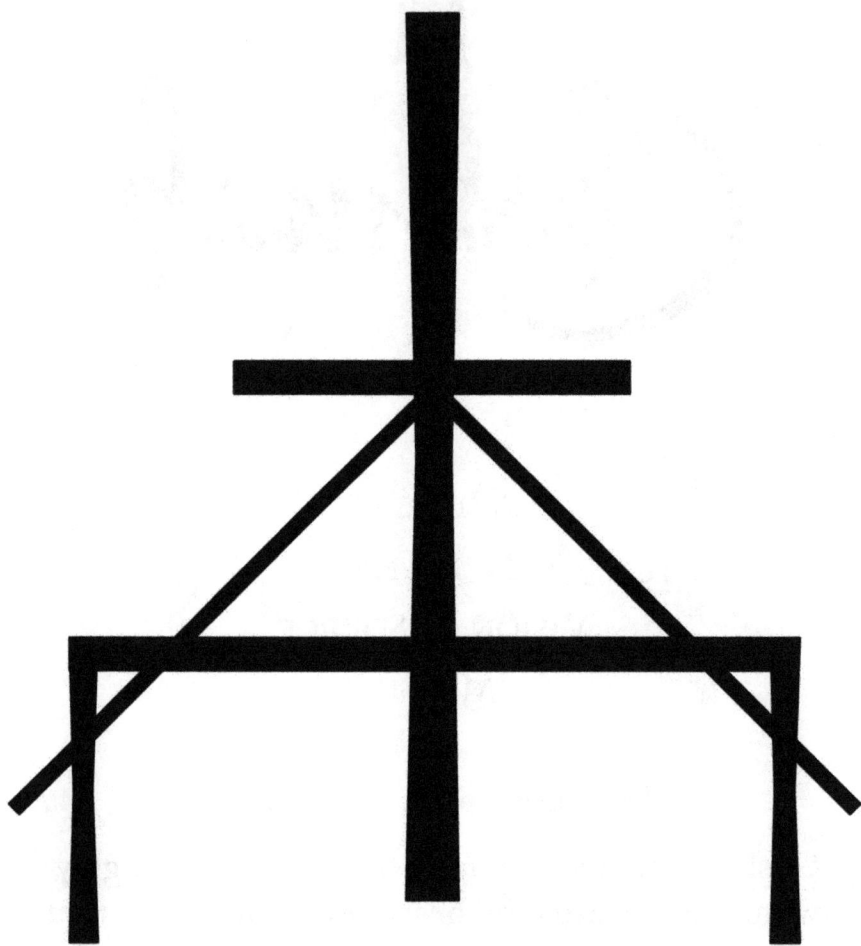

Path 11
to Kether

TRUMP 0

THE FOOL

URANUS

ALEPH

OX

Eternal Babe Dancing on the Edge of the Abyss
He who was goaded to come and play
in the Universe created and uncreated.
He who dares to speak the obvious.
He whose very folly brings infinite luck,
the baraka of the Wyrd.
Horned and fearless, self-contained and
guided by animal wisdom
He continually descends and climbs the mountain-tree
from which all Phosphorous Groves spring.
As it was. As it is. As it always shall be.

1
Kether

✣

CROWN

PLUTO

REUNION WITH SOURCE

IPSISSIMUS

THE VERY UTMOST SELF

All is the One.

One is the All.

All illuminated like a thousand candles.

All illuminated like a thousand lamps
suspended over the altar of sacrifice.

All illuminated like a thousands suns,
a thousand brilliant stars in the eternal now.

Echoing the dream of the song and the pattern of the
web, yet all is possible in the One.

Glossary

ABYSS: The separation between the higher three sephiroth of the Tree of Life, with the lower seven sephiroth. Within it is the "false" sephira of Da'ath or knowledge. The Abyss is the great challenge and trap to the magician seeking to climb the Tree of Life.

AEONIC: Referring to Aeons, or Ages, great epochs of time. Often considered the celestial "year" with various celestial "months" corresponding to Zodiac signs. We are currently on the cusp of the Age of Pisces and moving backwards to the Age of Aquarius. In Thelemic traditions, Aeons are marked by various Egyptian deities and we are currently in the Age of Horus, though possibly concurrent with the Age of Ma'at.

AKASHA: The fifth element. Spirit. Quintessence.

ALCHEMY: The art and science of transmutation. With forms from Asia, the Middle East and Europe, alchemy became a repository of esoteric thought and symbolism. It is focused upon the creation of the Philosopher's Stone and the Elixir of Life, which may or may not be one in the same. Some forms of alchemy are internal – psychological or bodily, while others focus on laboratory operations upon herbs, minerals and metals. Ultimately both are seeking the same thing and results in one world, inner or outer, will effect results in the other.

ANIMA MUNDI: World Soul or Universal Soul. The divine intelligence permeating everything.

APPLE: A fruit of immorality showing up in various myths, most notably the association of Avalon, Hesperides and the Garden of Eden.

BALMS: Healing herbs and the plant spirits generally well disposed to human contact.

BANES: Toxic herbs and the plant spirit that initiate Witches by bring them closer to the realm of spirits.

BAPHOMET: A divine figure made famous by a drawing from Elphias Levi depicting a human figure with a goat head, female breasts and a caduceus phallus and bat wings, sitting upon a globe. A candle is found between the horns and one arm points upward and one arm down, reminiscent of the As Above, So Below symbolism of Hermeticism, and upon his arms marked dissolve and coagulate, an alchemical maxim. Baphomet first appeared in the transcripts of the Templars trial, and was considered to be the secret mysterious god they worshipped, though no description or real evidence was provided. Baphomet was connected by Crowley as a possible reference to the Gnostic Abraxas deity, a similarly animalistic humanoid figure. Baphomet is also linked to Sophia, goddess of wisdom.

BARAKA: Blessing or Be Blessed. Possible Sufi origin of the Wiccan term "Blessed be."

BEAR: Symbol of both the Goddess and the Sacred King. Totem of the Star Mysteries of Bear Constellations and Polar Stars. King Arthur is a symbol of the Stellar Bear Mysteries.

BEGGAR: A "missing" major arcana card popularized by comic writer and occultist Alan Moore in his series *Promethea*. Considered to connect Da'ath with Chesed. The gods often took the form of beggars to descent from the heavens to interact with humanity.

CAMELOT: The Kingdom of King Arthur in the Grail Romance literature. Often a symbol for an evolved but imperfect realm upon the Earth striving for higher ideals than the society around it.

CHARIOT: Euphemism for a psychic vehicle crafted by a mystic to carry consciousness to more refined states of being. Also mentions of cauldrons, brooms, boats and wheels within wheels reference this vehicle. The *merkaba* or *merkavah* is its name from Jewish mysticism.

COPPER-GOLD: Orichalcum, a metal described by Plato said to be found in ancient Atlantis. Described as a rose-colored gold no longer available in today's world.

CROWN OF HUMILITY: The Fifth "hallow" in the Temple of Witchcraft, corresponding to spirit and service as a High Priest/ess. One must find/craft the Stone of Sovereignty, the Cup of Compassion, the Spear of Victory and the Sword of Truth before crafting the Crown of Humility.

DEVIL: One of the major arcana. In Christianity, the ultimate source of evil. In Witchcraft, bondage that one has agreed to, and only choice and action can we be freed from such bondage. That which challenges us and forces us to grow and become better.

DRAGON: A mythic creature that is an amalgam of all elements, like the sphinx. Sometimes a symbol of telluric energies of the Ley Lines. Sometimes a substitute totem for Aquarius or Scorpio. Also associated with the stars of Draco.

DREAD DOOR: The Gateway of Initiation. Can also be used to reference the Veil below Tiphereth, the Abyss below the three supernal spheres, or the threshold of the initiation circle where the initiate is challenged. In some initiation rites, also a symbol of the womb/tomb of the Goddess.

DREAD LORDS OF OUTER SPACES: Title of the Elemental Lords or Watchtowers in early forms of British Traditional Wicca. Some feel it is a references to alien consciousness similar to the forms described in the work of H.P. Lovecraft and Kenneth Grant.

FIVE-FOLD WORLD: World of the Five Elements and Senses.

FOUNTAIN: A "missing" major arcane card popularized by comic writer and occultist Alan Moore in his series *Promethea*. Considered to connect Da'ath with Binah. The flow of the cosmic ocean of Binah comes to us as an infinite fountain.

FOUR SQUARED CASTLE: The castle of the elements. An image of material creation. Associated with Chesed.

GALLOWS GOD: A form of the Witch god. Reminiscent of Odin or Wotan, who hangs from the World Tree to receive the mysteries of the runes. Gallows are associated with Witchcraft and the Mandrake.

GARDEN OF THE GODS: A term used in the Temple of Witchcraft to refer to the first time when al things physical and spiritual were in harmony, and a time we seek to recreate with our deeper knowledge earned from our separation.

GATE OF HORN AND IVORY: In Greek myths, dreams are sent forward through two gates, one of horn and one of ivory. Dreams through the gate of horn are true. Dreams through the gate of ivory will deceive.

HEDGE: A Craft image for the veil dividing flesh from spirit.

HESPERIDES: In Greek myth, an island to the west with a tree of golden apples, guarded by a snake named Ladon. Seeking the golden apples was one of the labors of Hercules in his quest.

ISHI BAHA: Said to translate to "fire that flows" and "water that burns." Used in the Cabot Tradition of Witchcraft as part of the sacrament of the Waters of Life, remembering Ceridwen's Cauldron of Inspiration and the initiation of Gwion Bach into Taliesin.

KNIGHT: The male questing aspect of the initiate.

LAW: The highest principle of Earth.

LEAD: One of the seven sacred metals. Associated with Saturn, karma and sin. Alchemist seek to transform the heavier metals such as lead into perfected gold, as they seek to transform their energy into enlightenment.

LEMNISCATE: Infinity loop associated with the various tarot cards.

LIBERTY: The highest principle of Spirit/Akasha. Often used as a replacement for Law in the Age of Horus, for the Law of the Age of Horus is Liberty.

LIFE: The highest principle of Air.

LIGHT: The highest principle of Fire.

LOVE: The highest principle of Water.

LOOM: The mechanisms of the universe. There are three wheels used by the Weaver goddess to make the universe and all in it – the Loom of Wyrd (Fate), the Loom of Ma'at (Justice) and the Loom of Tao (Judgement).

LUPINE: A type of flower. Also associated with wolves and wolf shape-shifters.

MALKUTH: The tenth sephira of the Qabalah. The sphere of Earth, the material universe.

MAGISTER: Master. Also referring to the grate of 8=3 in the traditions of the A∴A∴ and the Golden Dawn, the rank of Binah, or Master of the Temple, Magister Templi. Magister is also a title of the Master of a clan or group in Traditional Witchcraft.

MAGUS: Magician. Also referring to the grade 9=2 in the traditions of the A∴A∴ and the Golden Dawn, the rank of Chokmah.

MATER: Matter, also associated with Mother, the divine feminine.

MIGHTY DEAD: The Ascended Masters, Saints or Bodhisattva when viewed through the eyes of the Witch. Associated with Chesed and Binah specifically.

NAMER: In the Temple of Witchcraft, the middle self, the personality, ego and self identity of this current lifetime.

NIERIKA: The secret gate through which people pass through only at birth, death and dreams. Witches, shamans and sorcerers learn to pass through it at will and enter other realities. Drawn from the Huichol tradition. Sometimes associated with the back of the head where the skull and spine meet.

ORAN MOR: The Great Song of Creation, reverberating upon the strings of the Weaver's Web like a harp.

PARADISE: The Garden of the Gods. Zep Tepi. Eden.

PATER: Pattern, also associated with Father, the divine masculine.

PATH OF UNMAKING: The Crooked Path of the Witch. It unwinds the walker as we enter non-dual consciousness, or the Neither-Neither. Yet we have to craft ourselves, our souls, to get there, adding to the paradox of the path.

PENTAGON: A five sided shape. Symbol of the five elements, the terrestrial world and the Temple of Geburah/Mars.

PHOSPHOROUS GROVE: An image of Binah where every priest or priestess attaining this state is aflame with love and sorrow but will not burn. Similar to the City of Pyramids from Thelema.

PI: π – The infinite number of the Abyss, between three and four. Popularized by Alan Moore in his series Promethea.

POMEGRANATES: A fruit of immortality most strongly associated with Persephone, Demeter and Hecate in the Greek traditions.

QUEEN: The Goddess. The Divine Feminine. The Creatrix. The greatest mystery with both dark and light aspects.

ROSE: The flower of the western mystery tradition, as the lotus is to the East. Five petalled and sacred to the Goddess, particularly Venus figures. Sometimes depicted red, other times white, or depicted in conjunction with white lilies. A symbol of incarnation, death and protection. A variation of the pentagram or pentacle.

SACRIFICE: To make sacred. An offering freely given.

SHAPER: In the Temple of Witchcraft, the lower self, also known as the animalistic self, the primal self or child self. Connecting force between the Namer and Watcher.

SHE: English transliteration of *Sidhe*, the high faery creature of Irish myth. Equivalent to the *Sith* in Scottish lore.

SHE OF THE THREE WAYS: The Triple Goddess. The Witch Queen. The Goddess of the Three Fold Crossroads.

SIXTH SECRET DOOR: The Sixth Sense, the psychic faculty trained by sorcerers and witches.

SINGER: The God. The consort to the Weaver. He sings the Oran Mor which reverberates upon her webs. The Logos or Great Word.

SOVEREIGNTY: Reign. The Celtic Goddess of the Land in one of her many forms. The personal rulership that comes from service to the Land and Goddess, for the highest good of all involved.

SPHINX: A mythical creature composed of the Lion, Bull, Eagle and Human, the four fixed signs of the Zodiac (Leo, Taurus, Scorpio and Aquarius). Keeper and Guardian of Mysteries and the animal associated with Malkuth.

SUPER-NATURE: All of nature not categorized or recorded by the modern world. The mysteries of nature often unseen by the masses.

SWAN: Associated with the star mysteries of Cygnus, the ancestors and the psychopomps.

TERRA: A mystical name for the planet Earth.

TRUE WILL: The Mystic's Will. The desire of the higher self which all magicians seek to enact upon Earth. Life's purpose. The Heart's True Desire.

VESICA PISCES: Literally "fish bladder." The almond shaped symbol created by two overlapping circles. Also known as the Eye of God or Yoni, as well as a symbol of the fish in Christianity. From this form many other sacred geometric figures are derived, so it is considered a seed symbol for geometric creation. The Flower of Life geometry is based upon the Vesica Pisces.

VESSEL: Container. Also a symbol of the initiate and the initiate's consciousness.

WAND OF CREATION: A symbol of the cosmic phallus, the creative force of the Divine Masculine.

WATCHER: In the Temple of Witchcraft, the name given to the Higher Self, also known as the Bornless One or Holy Guardian Angel in Thelema and other forms of Hermetic Ceremonial Magick.

WAVES OF CREATION: The Nine Waves found in Celtic myth. Used in the Temple of Witchcraft to indicate the birth of nine orders of being that populate creation. The include the gods of the upper world, gods of the underworld, the gods of the middle world, the angelic orders, the faery folk, the spirits between, the stone people, the plant people and the creature of flesh and blood.

WEAVER: An image of the Goddess as the Goddess of Fate and Creation. She turns the looms and weaves the universe and the lives of all in it.

WITCH'S EYE: The Psychic Eye, Third Eye or *Ajna* Chakra, activated and functioning.

WITCH'S HEART: The Vessel for the True Will. Where one feels the Perfect Love and Perfect Trust of the Gods.

WITCHFIRE: The initiatory energy of consciousness associated with the traditions known as Witchcraft today. Can be equated with the fiery consciousness of other traditions, such as Kundalini.

WYRD: Fate determined by actions, not absolute destiny.

YONI: A symbol of the female genitalia, the holy feminine.

ZAZAS, ZAZAS, NASATANADA ZAZAS: The Invocation of the Abyss

ZEP TEPI: The time before in Egyptian mythology. Used synonymously with the Garden of the Gods in the Temple of Witchcraft.

About the Author

Christopher Penczak is an award winning author, teacher and healing practitioner. As an advocate for the timeless perennial wisdom of the ages, he is rooted firmly in the traditions of modern witchcraft and Earth based religions, but draws from a wide range of spiritual traditions including shamanism, alchemy, herbalism, Theosophy and Hermetic Qabalah to forge his own magickal traditions. His many books include *Magick of Reiki, Spirit Allies, The Mystic Foundation* and *The Inner Temple of Witchcraft*. He is the co-founder of the Temple of Witchcraft tradition and not for profit religious organization to advance the spiritual traditions of witchcraft, as well as the co-founder of Copper Cauldron Publishing, a company dedicated to producing books, recordings and tools for magickal inspiration and evolution. He has been a faculty member of the North Eastern Institute of Whole Health and a founding member of The Gifts of Grace, an interfaith foundation dedicated to acts of community service, both based in New Hampshire. He maintains a teaching and healing practice in New England, but travels extensively lecturing. More information can be found at *www.christopherpenczak.com* and *www.templeofwitchcraft.org.*

The Temple of Witchcraft
Mystery School and Seminary

Witchcraft is a tradition of experience, and the best way to experience the path of the Witch is to actively train in its magickal and spiritual lessons. The Temple of Witchcraft provides a complete system of training and tradition, with four degrees found in the Mystery School for personal and magickal development and a fifth degree in the Seminary for the training of High Priestesses and High Priests interested in serving the gods, spirits, and community as ministers. Teachings are divided by degree into the Oracular, Fertility, Ecstatic, Gnostic, and Resurrection Mysteries. Training emphasizes the ability to look within, awaken your own gifts and abilities, and perform both lesser and greater magicks for your own evolution and the betterment of the world around you. The Temple of Witchcraft offers both in-person and online courses with direct teaching and mentorship. Classes use the *Temple of Witchcraft* series of books and CD Companions as primary texts, supplemented monthly with information from the Temple's Book of Shadows, MP3 recordings of lectures and meditations from our founders, social support through group discussion with classmates, and direct individual feedback from a mentor. For more information and current schedules, please visit: *www.templeofwitchcraft.org*.